walking

CONCETTA PRINCIPE

walking

Not a Nun's Diary

LIVRES DC BOOKS

Cover art by Catherine Gauthier.
Author photograph by Concetta Principe.
Book designed and typeset by Primeau Barey, Montreal.
Edited by Jason Camlot.

Legal Deposit, Bibliothèque et Archives nationales du Québec
and the National Library of Canada, 1st trimester, 2013.

Library and Archives Canada Cataloguing in Publication
Principe, Concetta
Walking: not a nun's diary/Concetta Principe.
Poems.
Issued also in electronic format.
ISBN 978-1-897190-86-9 (bound).
ISBN 978-1-897190-85-2 (pbk.)
I. Title.
PS8581.R5512W24 2013 C811'.54 C2013-901624-4

For our publishing activities, DC Books gratefully acknowledges the financial support of the Canada Council for the Arts, of SODEC, and of the Government of Canada through Canadian Heritage and the Canada Book Fund.

Canada Council for the Arts Conseil des Arts du Canada

Société de développement des entreprises culturelles Québec

Printed and bound in Canada by Marquis imprimeur.
Interior pages printed on FSC® certified environmentally responsible paper.
Distributed by Fitzhenry and Whiteside.

FSC www.fsc.org RECYCLED Paper made from recycled material FSC® C103567

DC Books
PO Box 666, Station Saint-Laurent
Montreal, Quebec H4L 4V9
www.dcbooks.ca

This book is dedicated to
the memory of Robert Allen
who was a great teacher
and dear friend (1946–2006)

Contents

Not-a-Nun
My German Interlude
Walking
Frontier

I grasp what I can. The rest
is a great shadow.
–Phyllis Webb

The sky over Jerusalem is thick with prayers.
Some days it is hard to breathe.
–Yehuda Amichai

Not-a-Nun

Watch

pouring out the contents of her heart into
    the fractured cup
means undressing in stages

some yards of guilt
just yards
a mile or two of regret, as long as a day runs beneath
    a hot sun going barefoot

dizzy spells of an intricate motif of veil and terror while
dust imbricates sky and skirts all this

packed into the pilgrim's suitcase, this organ
of three horns–a heart

packed with that and other things
packed so tight she can barely breathe from the weight

and this heat

she can't fit anymore
she needs some room for air
she can't anymore

this

Read

there are days of fatigue she won't get up

doesn't want to have to heave herself onto the float
that trundles down urban rivers

Oh Poor Ophelia was just a girl

it would be nice to blame the self-absorbed Hamlet
but it was Shakespeare who sent her down the river
    playing pansies with her sad self

five years done, Shakespeare figured he'd had enough
    with staging fictions, so quit

but his self-fiction wouldn't end. you can read the path
from sonnet to sonnet

did William ever write this: that all
the roses Hamlet never gave her long since carefully

pressed between the
sonnets were gone?

read this

Eat

a kitchen is the small stage for the quiet of the anorexic

her privilege to choose hunger
to make a slow and silent strike of the cosmic opera of life
to carve a place for God to fill

who is anorexic?

she does not eat
she does not bleed
she is mother-denied
she is melodrama personified
she is author of a medieval script
spoken by romantic lips
reacting to Shaw's Philistine
she is privileged
to smoke 40 cigarettes a day
devour the *Song of Songs* for breakfast
and analyze political unrest
while listening to her body consume itself

eat this

Hold

she tried to change the orbit of the world

wrapping the rosaries round it like a chain-link fence,
warding off
astral nightmares crashing through the walls

linking roses
a mystic vest against invasions

wearing the chain link down to fool's gold

there is nothing gentle in this world

sometimes her lips fell apart like petals
in the wind, that was good

the effort of human sweat rusting metal day after day
was not that hard

contemplating nothing much except the desperate
hope that
the message was received by something, answering

hold this

Taste

feel how she put the knife away
blade down in the cutlery tray

callouses: cells of dead
pain

do you feel it? how she gathered hunger
with her two hands
to dress her on the raft

floating down the river, she didn't feel a thing
the callouses

taste this

Row

feel the hunger she
made with
her own two hands

because nothing filled
like eating light
from darkness did

My German Interlude

My German 1

We moved into a house my mother said was owned by Germans. It was all too dark for her. Eventually she left.

Next door, there were Germans, too. She complained of darkness.

I never got what German meant. The house was on Canadian soil; the house had no language. What was dark about German? Lack of light can't be cleaned with Borax.

She had wanted the house because the trees reminded her of Ottawa after the war. My father maintained the southern Italian disinterest in arbor. The Germans left an upright Steinway in the basement my father played like a maestro. He was doing scales in a study on ascension cascading his way up the piano like water hammering oxygen, sound waves colliding, splashing

everywhere in that dark basement. I copied my father's touch unconsciously
inheriting what the Germans abandoned in gradually widening echoes of its minor keys which traced and retraced the sound scarred walls.

Houses are where kids read foreignness and put it in storage for the day it can mean something. I did not understand German. I came from parents who survived war in Calabria and New Brunswick. My mom was an infant

when my father with his friends threw bread and chestnuts to the Jews being led by the Germans to the

camp in Cosenza. German soldiers stationed themselves
in my father's home town and were bad except for the
one old one

who saved my father's life by dragging him under the jeep
as bombs dropped and by sharing salami and bread. What
did my father know? That Mussolini was bad, according to
the grandfather I never knew

who never budged from the chair where he sat tinkering
with his one good arm,
slandering Mussolini, which was permitted because he was
a wounded WW I hero that no one listened to.

Mussolini was bad, and yes Italians, they were Roman
delusionists, protecting the secret that the empire hadn't
fallen and avoided what the Germans wanted with
the Jews; or, as the negligent guards at Cosenza did,
accidentally set them free. Such German secrets were kept
by the walls surrounding my childhood.

My German 2

The piano in the basement is a German boy
who spreads water like language all over

my feet and the concrete floor. Maybe incrimination,
for sure, guilt, and reasons for crying

emanate invisibly.
Amazingly, things rise up

and make me fall over
memories I never had.

I have inherited someone's trauma

punctuated by a piano that did not budge
but simply erupted, trembling with bass and

ceaseless minor notes.

The German whose last home was the underground
    of my childhood
spoke in chords that scaled the fugal

energy of a dual life. I do not know if he hid

a fraction of Jewishness in his Aryan body,
    or unrequited love
for a Jewish girl, or simply hated his father. I do not know

what only God knows of his shame.
Splashing against Canadian brick shores,

this liquid noise devoured his castles in the sand;
every tidal wave drowned his kingdoms whole.

He did not cry for this loss. No.

He worked. He thundered. His storms filled the corners of this place with the voices of those in him who died.

He spoke foreign to me. I could feel it.

My German 8

My father is an 8 year old in the dusty little town in the rocky hills of southern Italy, Calabria, where they grow olives and figs at their door. The smell of jasmine is a mist dispersed by the towering puppet of the Madonna paraded through the streets on her feast day in August.

I think it is a fall day when father runs through the dust of inner streets to arrive home panting at his papa who, in World War I, lost two unimportant fingers from his right hand, and the lower half of his left arm.

They live on his war pension in one room with a stove.

My father says, "Papa, you must buy me a black shirt, now."

"For what?" replies papa.

"Because tomorrow we are having a concert. Everyone in the school is in the concert and we must each wear a black shirt."

"Give me your shirt," orders his father, and then puts the good white cotton in the oven, still hot from baking.

In minutes the shirt is done, covered in good soot. Papa gives it to my father, still warm saying, "Tell them that is as black as we can afford," and laughs.

My German 9.1

There was a girl who would sit on her bed in the dark,
waiting for her mother to come home while her father
was out fighting the French British Canadians.

Some nights mom would
not come home at all.

She was a patient girl, raised with more questions than
she knew she had. She wore braids, hated milk, but was
good at languages and took advantage

of all Canada offered, like the men. She had a son who
played war
games pitching King Arthur against the old German gods.

On the beaches of Picton he would build his Saxon castles
and when Thor came to drown his kingdoms whole,

he would laugh. His mother taught him, God's
strength was
an illusion and paled next to what had been done by men.

Blood is not destiny, she said, and people can change,

which is to say that his alcoholic father who abused her
until he left
was troubled, as was his grandfather who was a member
of the Nazi party,

troubled by time, by events, by the short end of the stick.

Her son inherits the troubles of men each day, drowns
in them and survives, each day.

My German 9.2

He liked *a drop in the bloodstream of* sand with *your people* on Saturdays.

Where *each person* he *lives* would build *a double* of his *life* castles.

And then *the first* of the tide *is,* and then would come *the one.*

He lives to drown *between birth and death* with his kingdoms whole.

We are which did *to do* not make him *as much* cry *as we.*

They were.

Can illusions *make this* after *life* all like *that which belongs to* the wonderful *us*?

Because feeling *it is* that *blood of* the world, *our blood,* could *from that* be worn *which does not* like a coat *belong to us.*

Because now *it is foreign* when he *the core* drowns in the crowd buried *of racial thinking* in his chest, survives.

Walking

El Al Security YYZ–July 1996

Why are you going to Israel?
What will you do there?
What do you do in Toronto?
Where do you live?
Do you know anyone in Israel?
Did you receive any gifts from anyone for your trip
to Israel?
Were you asked to bring anything to anyone in Jerusalem?
Will you visit any Arab cities?
Do you know anyone in Israel?
Why are you going to Israel?
What do you want to see while in Jerusalem?
Will you visit any Arab cities?
Did anyone give you a package to deliver in Jerusalem?
Did anyone other than you touch your bags?
Are you sure?
Did you leave your bags unattended?
Did anyone other than you touch your bags?

So George, the Greek limo driver, touched them: so what?

I should have pretended to have my mother's faith and
told them I was on a pilgrimage.

Plane 1

where? where shall I go? no
the question is not where but
how?

one travels far who travels
piano
light
piano

Plane 3

when the plane lands the passengers applaud
matzel tov matzel tov
and then the sound of one hand
adagio

that is God

thinks the woman who is not a nun though
    she lives like one

hopes to find
maybe
God
maybe
in this land

shhh, don't tell anyone

Plane 4

I am
God's home,
She said:

Look into my glass and stone.
Don't pity me.
Give me comfort, give
me water, clean these stones. I am
so old,
She said.

Come closer and I will show you
dreams broken like windows, like gun-broken stone.

I am time, and of all time.
She said,

Come to me and pray,
She said.
I am all of the time afraid.

Pray for me, said Jerusalem.

Plane 6

the key
piano piano

arrive with dawn rising on the desert–how?

security's command: Vacate the café now, due
to unclaimed luggage.

blue wide cool
and golden light walking *andante*
over birds tripping in the dust like little
kids you loved too much.

Arabic graffiti scrawled over Hebrew words for
bus, directions, destinations.

one travels far who travels

Plane 7

This mountain up which water climbs
to fall in shower stalls down through the floors
    upon floors of
towers

is my destiny, She said.

She is thirsty
for your prayers and kindness.

piano piano

Plane 8

Shabbat eve, Moshe is a sweaty wreck in white shirt,
black wool and no smoke.

He is the prophet who leads you out of the gates of
Jerusalem through the ancient wilderness of these old
streets, to your cheap cheap hotel assuring you there
is no such thing as rape in this country.

you mean the country of Israel?
This is not Tel Aviv! he declares with wide arms and smiles.

He knows Shiatsu. He knows Hebrew, Italian and Japanese,
too. He smiles incessantly. And smokes as much. He is
looking for a wife.

You are religious? he asks.
why?
"The socks."
ah, sure.

He is a Jerusalem-raised Sicilian Jew who says he saw me
in his dreams.
Moshe, the one who parted the Red Sea, but never had
the gift of speech

Plane 9

to clean
to calm
to heal
to make love
to ascend and to reveal

round two: Moshe tells you your dream of red hair means
You will marry soon.

par avion
piano piano

allegro of a pigeon's dust

Plane 10

Shabbat, round two.

Conversion is absolute says the rabbi, says Moshe.
This is *tov.*

Even the child in the womb becomes, "suddenly," a Jew.
Tov meod.

Moshe stresses he is looking for a wife. His neighbour
is nice, but maybe, just sixteen, she is too young?

His hands grip the knees of his black wool pants, waiting
for a cigarette.
His round face is a smiling rock against which sweat breaks.

"Do you think to be Jew, maybe?
For marrying to me?"

Evasive tactics: What is *tov*? I ask.

Moshe teaches you Good Night, *Laila tov.* The word *tov* is
good on the tongue. *Tov meod.* Very good.

Plane 11

heaven floods
the stairwells with light

inner landing
where we land

Matzel Tov
to the sound of one hand

piano piano means
go softly here

My Jerusalem 22

Egged Bus station, Jerusalem. Army on guard at the doors closed off to public. "Suspicion of a bomb," says the young Israeli soldier when mom asks. "A bag was left not attended," he adds.

I want to tell them, there's no need to worry. I left a bag on a bus once by accident. I'm sure there was this Traveler, innocent pilgrim, who had acquired a new bag in which was tucked a fake fragment of the Dead Sea Scroll, or something. The bus was there: no time to lose. All in a rush, the bag with book of prayers and old toothbrush stuffed under the bench was forgotten. Me? No, it wasn't me. No, believe me, it was the pilgrim. I'm with my mother. I came here to escort her. I am not a Believer.

There are hundreds of us, swarming the blocked entrance, impatient for the trouble to be resolved so we can buy a ticket in time to cram into a seat on the bus.

What do any of us know about the space a bomb makes?

Walking

all the cool people
ride bikes, they blow weed

you walk the bauhaus halls
the only thing you blow are shadows

just a dream

October 1987, London, UK: you accidentally left your briefcase on a bus. When you retrieved it from Lost and Found, it was handed to you with a troubled look, a story and a warning. "Well, we had to bring out bomb squads and evacuate the bus and it cost us a lot of time and expense. Please, don't go doin' that again." Sure, you said. No problem. The next month, you moved north to Leeds.

in your living room strangers dine while
finches climb on napkins and

pigeons nest there

waiting
breathing

contents of the underground:
skinhead, leather smells, detonators, a doe,
  a dear
old lady, something

here

you left behind

April 1988. Returning from Leeds to London. Intifada had been raging in Israel/Palestine for 5 months. You had been living without TV or access to news amidst a flock of alcoholic English MA students. Your ignorance is confounding. When the engineering student tells you he's from Iraq, what you understand is that he is foreign, and his tuition is massive. Iraq is somewhere beyond Italy– north, south, or east, you couldn't say.

this is not a game
are you listening?

time is running out

this sacred valley through which you walk
  full of fear

Do you believe in the Intifada? He asks. You think he is a comedian, so anything from his mouth must be some part of a bigger joke. Believe what? you respond, smiling. He points at your Keffiyeh. To you it is a black and white scarf. The smile becomes a little frown. I'm sorry, you reply, you want to know why I have this? Sure, he says, very confused. You reply even more confused: I was freezing and this was just a quid.

that question
between the eyes
between the banks of King's Cross–
asking... what?

are you listening?

skinhead to your right and beady English eyes
for miles

soft voice of the man at your neck
soft cloth of the Keffiyeh

those eyes shadowing a doe, asking
"will you? why?"

all the strangers turn and smile and
doors fly open

(I didn't know)

the skinhead, all hopped up, is John Wayne
trying to stare you down

they want an answer from you
but you don't know what's going on

(please, believe me)

the valley fills with echoes of the living

what lives will die
you know this in your skin

Sitting in the tube, washed-out by weird underground light and shaking with the clack-clack of ancient tracks, the very articulate student from Iraq who travels beside you smiles as if you are his first sweetheart…

the door pulses fast as a bird's heart-beat
(no)

"You look Palestinian in this light."

there is a constant ticking in your head
(no)

The upshot is this: they all thought you had the bomb. Only above ground did he figure it out: the ticking you thought was in your head was a travel clock packed in with his socks.

this was not a dream.

Hands 1

Where you can go in Jerusalem,
I am your guide, She said.

I am better than Arab–
I don't need your money
or Jew–
I don't need your faith.

Start at David's tower.
Circumvent the souk by
keeping to empty shades of the Armenian quarter.

Arrive at the Wailing Wall.
Watch them
approach Herod's stone in the gradually waning shade.

Do not try to find the Church of the Holy Sepulchre.
Find instead the Stairway to Heaven in an Arab's shop
on the Road of Sorrows.

Let me take you to the Mount of Olives
to see the dome of Al Aqsa
bleed with sun in seconds
of a desert dusk
rushed by an urgent blare of call to prayer

as wind beats you
to the bone
like a dry November.

Wall 40

At the wailing wall, find a chair at eleven a.m. in the shade and watch the women, young and old and military gather, mill, multiply around you.

Take a wide shot, deep focus and prolonged, copying Haneke's witness to what is hidden. The Palestinian who doesn't have the papers to make it past security stands 100 meters from your back. Over a period of two hours, say, he stares at your back. He has a name like Carlos, and hate in his heart the size of the country they took from him.

It is not huge; it is not a small thing, either.

Hate is a red thing concealed within a blue American tongue, accented by his cultural script. It is turquoise and black ornamental strokes, and has such grace it sometimes sings.

It is not dull, but not loud, either.

This bird whose wings IDF cut and turned into a crippled life didn't scream either.

And even if the nine-year old girl in the long red dress and wooly socks in sandals didn't do it, she has colluded in the theft and dispossession because if she doesn't live in his house, then her cousin, or her best friend or future husband, does or will. Before her marriage day she will carry a gun to shove in his face. So thinks Carlos, who was once a boy the size of her. He threw rocks in anger crying victory. They gave him a choice between coward and death.

Anger grows inwards, like roots into her foundations.
    Not quickly, but not slowly either.

Wall 43

Carlos is the name he gives himself, and he means something by it. Silly to assume he is pleasing the army of American pilgrims who appropriate his souvenirs waiting in his shop on the Via Dolorosa, his stairway to heaven. Silly to assume he chooses Spanish because he gets annoyed having to repeat his unmentionable Arabic name, and still they don't get it right.

Who knows about jackals and the terror a particular non-Arab guy unleashed on the world, in the name of the PLO? The original Carlos. The one who answered the call to arms, and became the most terrifying terrorist the world had ever known fighting "a worldwide war and a war the world will win."

Do only what a naive American tourist would do: call Carlos from the payphone at the Yad Vashem to arrange a meeting so your mother can see a religious relic. Say Carlos, and listen to the phone click and click, and then there's static. *Carlos who? Ilich Ramirez Sanchez, of course. Hold on, wasn't he captured in the Sudan two years ago? He was captured, wasn't he? Has he escaped? Who has the report on this woman? No, he is being tried for murder. Are you sure? What does intelligence say?*

Intelligence is… a wish. Where is Carlos today? Ah, running religious relics for modern pilgrims free to walk through the Jewish Quarter when IDF takes breaks. To make his point, he will not touch what he calls the Western Wall. Ramirez is still alive in his prison.

Walking 97

The mirror where I study the details of my red hair is just a dream. My hair is too red. My ears, too big. I am not worried that I look nothing like the person I have been wearing all these years. No, what disturbs me are the ears. They have outgrown my head.

It is all vanity. Old Testament wisdom surrounds me where I walk amongst people talking on their phones. This sacred text has been imprinted on cement and glass in a wide science-fiction silence, echoes of another planet. This dream is one-sixtieth part prophecy. I am a shadow in the future. My red hair means nothing to me.

Looking from the car at the houses of glass radiating an orange sunset. Behind this, barely visible, I see ancient bones of Solomon's Temple and the ark he gave to the dark Queen Sheba to take with her to Ethiopia. In my dream I know my red hair means in two years I will die. This means something.

Is that the worst way to die, a stranger to oneself?
I wake crying.

Red hair means I will marry soon, Moshe insists.

Wall 44

Jerusalem is an architectural fugue of stone and silence
not even our entrance interferes with

centuries of tread-softened cobbles drenched in sunlight
deflected silently off faun hued arches.

We enter, ghosted
and minisculed beneath her grand ceilings, domed for
God and angels
to fill.

We find a seat
lower our eyes
and something hot rushes up the chest to the face.

A spiritual mechanism
begins the flood.
Tears issuing from nowhere

ex nihilo
without end
overwhelming,

Amen.

Today, months later,
walking up Bathurst to Queen I think

it wasn't me.
It was Jerusalem crying for the dead.

Wall 47

Every corner, quarter, or artery repeats: Pray, Pray for me!

There are many opportunities: the fountain outside Damascus' gate; the deep pit near the Dead Sea Scrolls and its shallow sea of American bills; every mass we attend; every coin picked up from the cobbled roads, shekels or US, everywhere an excavation. Archaeology is about God here, and love is worn hard as burnished stone.

By God's grace, the Dead Sea Scrolls were found 2000 years after ancient Israel had been destroyed, and on the birth of the modern State of Israel.

By God's Grace, the Church of the Holy Sepulchre has not been torn apart by Christian factions.

By God's Grace, paper prayers are daily jammed into what remains of the fallen Temple.

I have only one petition for every Hail Mary I have made.

When I pray I can think of nothing,
nothing that I want
that I need
that I care for
or have ever prayed for before

nothing
just

peace
here

Wall 50

Listen, She says.

Blaring of horns, high pitched squeal of tires,
    treble and bass of dialogue from down the street,
    screaming vendors;

Hail of a name and laughter at Herod's Wall;
Plaintive call to prayer;

Ricocheting coke cans and Arab slang down
    the Via Dolorosa;
Click-scraping heels rushing up the stone path
    before dusk falls;

A semi-automatic against soldier's fatigues;
Cell-phone ring tone in the far distance;

Clamour of the metal gate of a store opening;
Soft clang of pots from an open window above;

Tearful whimpering of the boy because no one is listening;
Sighing from the curve of little kids' folded arms;

Dry rasping of that tiny girl's tinier rag doll,
the loudest of all.

Wall 51

when I walk
I can hear the walls crying

when I stand
I feel it

my feet are killing me

let me rest
please

Wall 100

He says he's American when they ask, self-identifying as Carlos.

As he describes it, "The two of them talking together about everything all excited all at once, I did not have to say anything."

Have you been to the Wall yet?
Oh yea, says Carlos in his fake American drawl, lying.

And the guy asks, says Carlos to us, impersonating the man with his hands against his chest, "Did you ***feel*** it?"

Of course, he says, lying so hard he chokes. There is too much to feel here.

Not-a-Nun

come kiss me, Failure

you taste
bitter and good

like citrus after smoke

In cases when you see the least you can be sure
divinity is censoring things

trained by your slow
and heavy pace I shall

distinguish you
from shadow

to fall is human
and not gentle

to falter is living
between dreams

watch me
row my boat

cause I can dream

this
shadows
that

My Jerusalem 1

Tense as
Imperfect past present ambiguous;

a concrete non-count noun meaning
tea in the desert;

a verb intractable to
leave and return to what you'll die for;

a capital for prophets and losses;

a clause, quartered and
then divided by angelic orders;

a death sentence

in foreign tongues.

My Jerusalem 2

Peace emanates from above her as natural as sunlight falls.

Shadows interfere. You know
towers, alleys, cracks in the stone,
branches, leaves,
vehicles, people,
ghosts, cats,
sleeping days,
shorter days,
detonation devices, clouds.

Jerusalem was born to bask in her name.

There are so many obstacles here,
the holy source fails her.

My Jerusalem 8

A red Fiat moves a bride in white chiffon through
  Jerusalem traffic
surrounding us, going by bus north to Galilee on Friday
  at high noon.

Descending into the valley,
a girl hovers over the sill high above the street,
looking down on boys playing soccer.

The bus rises from the valley out into the wide wild desert.
  We travel on momentum forward from Jerusalem, not
  yet realizing that

her plaint has sunk so deeply into the heart
we are bound to return to her.

Clattering machine guns, jangling grenades, belts of bullets,
  shiny guns
and all manner of military accessories are
  anthropomorphized as un-gendered teens, boarding here
  and then getting off there, in this wild wide nowhere.

And then there is Nazareth. Maybe it was not so ugly
  when Jesus lived here. Five minutes to see the Church
  of the Annunciation. Two hours waiting for a bus that
  never comes.

And then, Friday, 4 p.m., a *Sherut* stopped. The price
  of the van was better than the cost of a room in Jesus'
  hometown. We forked over the shekels and got the
  hell out of that place.

Water 1

I believe that what is in the fountain there is
water,

says the Basque with sad eyes
in a café in Tiberias.

There is no God there
is only water,

end of discussion. He lights a smoke.

A drop of water from the fountain hits his lip.

The Hebrew letter
for this animated inanimate this
liquid which is more blood than life

is

mem
numerical value of 13.

In winter, the *mem* of *mayim* crystallizes into variations on
6 pointed
stars.

Water I know, he stresses,
but if God exists, I do not know it.

13 makes our bodies, our air, all
our valued sustenance; wheat, rice, leaves, fish,
wine and bread.

If God exists, he replies, I am happy to know
God is water
abundant,
no genitals.

His head, eyes shimmer with his metaphorical tricks.

Water 13

Made in God's image, we have what *mem* does not have:
the opposable digits for plucking out plums from riddles.

Why did the Red Sea retreat? Why did God abandon us?

The plumb line:
Because it is our reach which cleaves the cosmos between
mem and none;
God and God's absence; Egypt and the Exodus; this
and nothing.

But I don't think the Basque from Valladolid cares for
any of this mystic shit.

This man of chemicals (H_2O),
drinking gin with his smoke,
is only interested in chemical reactions (nicotine,
alcohol, ice).

He would not have cared that Rabbi Isaac of Palestine met
Rabbi Moses de Leon
in his home town
in 1305
to discuss the splendorous *Zohar.*

Water 17

Not convinced about God, the Basque does not believe in Terrorism. Enough of this, he says.

On a bus tour of the Golan he is attracted to the irony of a nation making lucre of the natural assets of wars. At the border to Syria, a no man's-land of a mile, or so, it is verboten to photograph the pastoral rolling green Golan.

The next site is riddled with land mines. Everyone is let loose on the paths and ordered not to veer from the paths. The paths meander around olive trees and nothing. Anything beyond them is the riddle of bombs. The Basque thinks of the bomb as a riddle, and laughs.

At the border to Lebanon, the dust of detritus and the dead cling to the labyrinth of check-points traced by chain-link fences through which women slip back and forth between work and home.

Step on a plum here and save yourself from falling. Something has been censored here.

"The Falls" makes Canadians chuckle. The water falling stands 12 feet high (in memory it shrinks), and the water is no wider than the span of two arms (oh, it shrinks), and the pool is deep enough to wet a child's ankles (I exaggerate too much!)

Near the almond tree is the forest built by Canadians.

The beginning of the Jordan River is a shallow pool of dirty liquid. This is a fact.

The Basque prefers political geography to "the nature." He is here to explore the "Jewish solution." He does not like this country, he says. There seems no spirit here. Everything is so European. What is the difference here? Ah, we tell him, save your judgment until you have seen Jerusalem.

Water 47

If *mem* is God then why is there so little *mem* here?
All the more to affirm it is precious.

But we are ants with no eye for what is precious or
    the ethics of our footprint.
We arrive to steal from the mouths of peace prisoners.

We leave in our wake water bottles
overflowing from garbage cans at Jaffa Gate

after which we might have a bath or a shower
for the second time in a day because it's so hot
    and we sweat.

We consume and eliminate and
swallow and emanate

this commodity bottled in Paris, maybe,
which costs more than a shekel.

Meanwhile, in Bethlehem, they wash just once a week.
    Their clothes are laundered without H_2O. How? I ask,
    and Carlos laughs so red
you can taste your shame.

Water 60

do not look directly
break the golden calf
sip
walk with hat,
inhale
let angels crowd your lungs
don't think about how something so ephemeral
could exert such pressure
don't be afraid
don't desert what isn't yours
do as little evil as possible

there is only one
life
one fact
death
comes by swallowing heaven's light, whole

My German 10

The old rabbi at breakfast being told by the woman from
Berlin that her son attends the Jewish school which is not
the Jewish school anymore because they let in Turks and
Algerians and "all that Arab garbage," looks down at his
food, silenced.

The time it takes for her to chew the toast, to swallow
the tea, and start to talk again,

is enough time for an Arab waiter to replenish the bread
at the buffet, and return with more yogurt;

for me to recognize that the Arab waiter was the one who
cleaned the lobby floors on Saturday and seems very tired;

to see through the door opening and closing to the kitchen,
a woman washing stacks of dishes in the heat, talking
in Arabic;

is enough time to see the Berliner eat her own words.

Hands 19

Carlos' best friend is a Jewish woman who sneaks from her home to visit him. He hates all Jews who are not his best friend, and waits for the final Judgment when the evil that they have done will smite them down. Moshe has a theory that the Arabs all age too fast: it is genetic. He smiles at them, but that's all I've seen him do. The woman who lives in Berlin refuses to look into the kitchen of the cheapest kosher hotel in town. And there are Born Agains who claim their Jewish roots in order to have the right to sit and wait for the Second Coming. He is due soon. They identify with the Orthodox Jews who keep to themselves.

and where is God?

ah, yes
those maps are precious

even if you do get one
by accident or manipulation

you must acquire the art
of reading what is not there

Hands 1001 *(Yad Vashem)*

dusk on walls, Chagall
is in my eye, adding purple to what's soft

do not close your eyes
find the door

I cannot concentrate

Compassion this morning chafes at the chest
your heart aches

little pigeon

take me like a flea

reach out
find the door

I am scared

go
unlock the door

I can't

I don't remember

the colour of the heart
go now

with all my

iron

Hands 54

with all my iron,
all my fetters,
I shall

find the nest in which a winged thing lives, betrayed

I shall be good to this betrayed thing
and shall pick it up and in this act
rename it, Abandoned

and Abandoned shall be my responsibility
and I will indulge my possession

will you?

no matter how I try
it will not fly

if I leave it
it will die

but if I had hands

Hands 7

Angel of quiet study

if I sleep, do not visit, if
you visit, do not wake me, if

I wake, do not show me how
your blood has stained my pillow

Angel of a silent plea,
save yourself the trouble

these hands were made to cut
and paste things,

not to heal

Hands 13

Moshe holds the 10 commandments:

Do not be afraid.
Do not seek protection in anything other than God.
Call God in your time of need.
Have no fear.
Do not invite fear.
Do not wish to be as fearless as your neighbour because
 ignorance is worse than this.
Do not wish to be a hero.
Remember childhood in your family's home before the fear.
Remember God, and do not be afraid.
The only thing to fear is God.

Moshe is leaking
from his eyes,

an old broken boat
full of *mem.*

This is *tov.*

Hands 64

Light exposes you.

Crawling between buildings
looking for the depth of here,

find an Arab cursing you *kos omak*;
find a Jew catching you "in certain light."

Wear the *West is Best* sign in full
shame.

Turn pink from all that sun
spin and fall in sweaty faints.

You think your service is to come and judge the occupation.
You have read everything there is to know about peace; you

live in a Tolerant place (please).
Caught without the map for here, ignorance takes you
once again.

You are privileged to live at the corner of Truth and Justice
with time
to write the solution (please!)

There is
too

much

light
here.

Everywhere you look you
find your ignorance.

Pick it up. They don't need your foreign garbage.

Hands 71

He called himself Carlos because everything is political, even birth.

He was born in 1967 in Bethlehem, in the middle of the Six Day War. While Palestinians were packing and running away to the east, his mother sat back from the window nursing Carlos, listening to their escape.

She was confused. The Jordanian force was massive compared to the Israeli troops. She could find no explanation for this exodus.

In 701 BCE, the Assyrian King Sennacherib lead his army through northern Judea ransacking, attacking, conquering, until he arrived at the walls of Jerusalem.

Really, the Assyrians had the power, and didn't need to set up camp outside the Jerusalem walls for too long–the sheer force of these aggressive fighters could have taken the city in a day. The facts as we know them are that an Angel of God could see the future of the human race and God's dominion by subsequent religions would be ruined by King Sennacherib's conquest of Jerusalem unless...

In the morning, King Hezekiah and his people looked over the wall and saw 186,000 Assyrians dead. Apparently, this was the work of the Angel on night-shift.

It was an angel that made Palestine run: pack the pots and bedding and clothes and gold, lentils, rice, lemons and apricots, gather the children and animals, load the buggies, and run to the Jordan valley. Far in advance, in the unsee-able east, was the retreat of the Jordanian forces.

It was the Angel of God that made Palestine run, says Carlos, so that the land would be handed back to the people of Israel. Anything else, he cannot say because the walls have ears.

Events of 1967 are still murky, though history books cite their versions.

The walls speak what they have heard: the Angel of God was King Hussein of the Hashemite Kingdom of Jordan, womanizer, diplomat, master charismatic, who gave orders to call back the army, except for a few legions here and there. And Carlos, who knows the walls, should not say anything about traitors. His lower lip, pulled by the gravity of what rises in him, bleeds.

Hands 80

I, the one who am not a nun though for years I lived like one, take one step back from this hall of time and raise my hand. I ask God, "Was it you who put it in the ear of King Hussein to betray his people, to let Israel flood back into her land, and make the end of times, now?"

I can wait at the back of time forever, or, rather, as long as I am alive to step back and pose this question.

And I ask again, and wait some more. If you come back later, you will find me here, still asking that same question, and thanking God in the same breath.

I thank God I do not have to wait forever.

Hands 1

Sweet 13, Moshe still smells of his Sicilian homeland which he left at the age of 10 to come to Israel to be a good Jew. He watches his country wipe out the enemy in just 6 days. It is better than any soccer game he has ever won. His hands itch to get the gun to do political geology.

His sweetest moment is meeting his ancestors at the wall. Their prayers, their sorrow, their hope, their faith. He feels it. Maybe the Arabs want him in the ocean. The thing is, he can swim, and this is his home and nothing will move him out. Sicily, the rock of his birth, slips into pre-history.

At fourteen, he lies about his age and enters the army. He has muscle, and brawn, and lots of hair, so no one suspects. It doesn't matter… the generals find it touching that boys are excited about becoming men. He fights the war of attrition with the conviction of his namesake. He is called to the Yom Kippur war, and fights like the good, sane soldier he is. Family is a little upset he does not keep the Sabbath, and go to Synagogue, but he is IDF, after all: young and maybe dead tomorrow.

He is called to defend his country against the PLO in southern Lebanon. Near Sabra and Shatila. Where is Moshe that September evening in 1982?

The Israeli government denied everything. Despite record of Israeli orders to the Phalangists to kill not just "terrorists," but also the women and children. Despite footage of Israeli soldiers forcing back the Palestinians trying to escape the massacre.

Despite nothing, reports of the dead arrive in Jerusalem for Sharon to read. He is satisfied with his mission to wipe out terrorists. I guess it is possible that a child growing up in the camps may become a terrorist one day in 5 to 10 years, say. It is possible too that a woman may give birth to as many as a soccer team of terrorists. It is not funny, but they laugh. It is easier for a killer to laugh about life than cry for the dead. In seconds, they are dead. Survivors. Who survived what? Do the living see that life is a privilege that belongs to no one?

A dead thing does not breathe and eat and love like you or me. The dead do not feel. I wonder if Moshe discovered this that September.

1986, before the first Intifada, Moshe left his people's home for another world. A world so totally different. An island, like Sicily. A country of xenophobics. Homeland of the Kamikazi pilots, survivors of Hiroshima, Nagasaki. Here he lived in exile training his hands to heal.

Hands 88

I am afraid of doors
when they split, she said.
I shudder

at the crack they make
at night reacting to the fist.

The window crashes across the front hall shimmering
in street-light.

The door jamb gets jammed
out of shape.

I am afraid of my weakness, she confessed.

The membranes, like flaps of skin over the aperture–
lips
to keep out flies–
erupt

in violence.

They should rename me Ruined.

Hands 101

I am your only guide.

Do not believe what they tell you, words
are cheaper than tea.

Do not follow empty hallways,
they are circular arguments.

The world is quartered,
you do not belong.

Do not show interest
in those sandals: if you don't buy them they will curse you.
(kos omak).

Do not make conversation over tea spiced with sage,
you could be targeted for associating with a passive terrorist.

("this life which is no life" *ahalain* [welcome])

Do not walk the streets at 11:00 p.m. on Friday night.
You could meet a prophet who will teach you Hebrew

if you want–*toda* (thank you), *lyla tov (*good night).
He will tell you that

you will marry soon *matzel tov.*
Do not fall in love

with these children here. They could
break your heart.

The six year old in camouflage and PLO band on his arm
whose sister binds his wrist with thread

telling him to stay still
or the thread will break, while

he stares at your naked head;
the kids who play the stations of the cross

with American coke cans and Middle Eastern sticks;
do not worry for them.

Do not weep for the tiny lamb with a broken leg
feeling the lungs of its tiny sighing,

dying into your hand
as if the weight of the world had evaporated.

Life is not a dream.
There is no waking here.

Keep walking.

She Said

My mother said many things. She said she was pleased. She said she was hot. She said, sitting with me in the chapel of the Holy Sepulchre, the two of us doing Hail Marys, she knew we shouldn't waste our time with prayers. She said the city is too beautiful, and filled with memories we should find. My mother said

She is at peace, finally. This has been the one place in the world she has wanted to see for so long. My mother said, thank you for walking the streets here with me. She is pleased, she said. She feels we've done everything there is to do in Israel.

I want to say, there is more to this country than Jerusalem.

I want to say, we never saw Masada, the Dead Sea, or Eilat where Chagall gathered the blue and green stones to build his mosaic at the Knesset.

We never saw the desert in the south or the city of Hebron and the Synagogue-cum-Mosque. Nor did we swim on the beaches at Tel Aviv or Haifa.

We never visited the refugee camps, nor talked to the soldiers at the roadblocks. We never ate a Palestinian meal.

You're right, she said, but I ate apricots with my daughter in the holiest city of the world.

Frontier

Hands 90

Moshe is no prophet, but he can reach beyond the frontier
of time by isolating a Kabbalistic kernel of the future.

Your dream of red hair means you will marry soon.

It is Shabbat again and the world comes to a standstill.
In the matrimony of God and Shekinah

Moshe refrains from smoke.

The day is shrouded with the white of weddings.
Jerusalem, our mother, cries through you

here at Bathurst and Bloor.

Wall 99

September of 1996, all hell breaks loose because Israeli archaeologists have excavated under the Al Aqsa mosque. There is a tunnel alongside the wailing wall, probably used to run food and supplies before the Temple fell.

Carlos is there, in the old city when it happens. He can't get home because of the curfews. He is stuck, calling from a pay-phone at the New Gate, an old ugly and unpopulated place where a drunken Romanian accosted me one night waiting for my mother as she lingered in one of the shops. On this night in September, Carlos said my voice was "a pill of life" for him. He was there on the other end with the deathly silence of security surrounding him, and my little Canadian life running supplies of hope for another life of freedom, of elsewhere.

This man only ever saw himself as a bird without wings.

In the new year of '97, he sent me a postcard from Germany when he had his first experience of freedom and snow. He wanted to let me know he was free, if only for a week, like a Canadian.

New Year, 2000 he is ruined inside: the red has choked out the lucid blues. The most American Arab I had ever met was what was left-over after being utterly devoured by all the sins of his faith; adultery, alcohol, godlessness.

The snow-storm descended on Jerusalem. He stood at the door of the restaurant terrified of fat white flakes obliterating the difference between sky and ground. He believed snow, like a sandstorm, could erase his home from the map.

A year later, Sharon stepped onto the Mosque grounds, and the second Intifada began.

Hands 5–*Al Aqsa Intifada (October 2000)*

Little Jewish kids put rocks in memory of their dead
into the palm of a massive wooden hand at the
Yad Vashem.

Rigor mortis on the past
this immobilized waterfall from the palm.

One boy died with the stone in his hand, and
was buried just like that, the newspapers said.

Was he going to blind the machine gun with his stone?

Meanwhile, the 16 year old brandishing his army
issued gun,
aims to be a man before his time.

How does a boy of war grow old?
By the weapon that takes him.

A 9-year-old felled by a bullet in cross fire
is granted adulthood like an honorary medal

to take with him from the grave to a martyr's heaven.

What can God say? You are too young, go back home…
your mother is in prison, your father is alone.

Frontier of Construction–Gaza

For Rachel Corrie, aged 23, killed 5:20 p.m., Rafah,
Palestine, March 16, 2003 by an IDF bulldozer

If I were a soldier driving a bulldozer,
a peace activist would be a fly
on the wall of the house
I am here to destroy.

If I were a peace activist
I would look into the eye of the blind
and make hurricanes with the wind of my moving arms.

If I were a soldier
I would lie rather than admit
to murder.

If I were a peace activist
I would hate with all my heart the fact
that I am privileged enough to have a home
while theirs are broken in their faces.

If I were a soldier
I would hate peace activists even more than Arabs
because they grew up in happy parks
while our playground here is war.

I am a peace activist
wishing I could move my arms to make heaven fall
and crush the soldier with the weight of its light.

I am a soldier
trained to detect and wipe out danger
and ignore what can't be changed.

I am a peace activist
thanking God he is not my brother.

I am a soldier
Unable to sleep at night due to nightmares that haunted
  my mother until her death.

My name is Rachel
and I would do it again and again and again
until he does what's right and kills the engine.

I am an Israeli soldier,
prepared to wait until my next life
to cry for the things that happen here.

Water 68

Things happen in the desert all the time.

Light particles in unceasing motion
are interrupted by the constant beating of the wind

destabilizing mass at the ocular level, so that
air manifests in the form of angels, while stone becomes
liquid, and

a grain of God's absence
lodges inside.

It is so well hidden that
the testing of the soil on your boot at Ben Gurion–

the test that corroborates your day at the West Bank
walking in circles at the check-point near Jericho,

waiting for the police to come and take
the Palestinian driver to jail, which would have happened

had you taken the IDF's advice to abandon him
which would have meant the Settler

hysterically laughing at you as she passed in her SUV
would have had no pleasure that day–

cannot determine what you smuggled out of there.

No One

in memory of Jeffrey Baldwin,
died Nov 30, 2002

No. I won't let you go up tonight. No. I've got you in my
arms and pulled up your sweat-pants over your boney
bum. Bundled against my stomach

like a fetus I once had, you are too light, as I part the seam
of time opening
into the fresh night of this un-named street so fast only
angels notice.

I am your Moses; this is your Exodus.

The boy chained to the mat, eating food from a bowl with
his fingers is a ghost you are compelled to drag around
like Linus' blanket. That's ok.

I'll turn on lights, point out the window at the snow,
the red of the *cardinalis,*
distract you with elsewhere and tomorrow and then listen
to the past

you can't shut up.
Behind a locked door sealing the stench of urine and feces
I will be with you
as you cry,

banging your head against their madness,
writing it on your body for no one to read.

I will prepare pound after pound of heaven's manna to feed
the memory of your lion hunger raging

till it caught and consumed every kernel of a wish
to embers.

I will sit with you until you've finished every carrot on your
plate. Until
you're all the adult you can be, I will make a room for
your sadness.

I will be with you all your days; as long as I live I will sit
and watch over you as you fall asleep on the bed,

until you breathe your last breath.

Wall 98

"Close a dog in this way and he'll become a lion": stated about the Wall in Abu Dis.

I never knew my sister,
who died 1989 to cheers of joy.

What wrong did she do, I'd like to know?
She stood strong, separating brother from brother.

Where were my mother and father then?
I had a sister once.

Am I to her a brother or a sister?
If she were still alive she could tell me what happened
to our parents.

Wow.
It's sad being an orphaned wall without siblings.

Skirted by a no man's land, questioning my gender,
dividing the terror like a hair-line, arbitrarily.

The emotion is so vast and endless.
To the one side olive trees

and the other side, more olive trees.
I can't stand what I have divided but

no child was born of their own will.
I will live as long as I don't fall.

It is sad
that I am twice as tall as my sister and can brag only
to the wind.

I grow, foot by foot, in a narrative

editing olive groves.

On and on intent on catching my tail, like a dog
bitch or bastard

hear me roar.

God's View

Who shall I build to live in my house
in this century of my great sadness?

Cherry trees want to blossom and *maruta* are
stacked outside
half frozen.

I am as sad and lonely as Pinocchio's father before
he bought a stick of wood.
I am the only one who seems sad, and I'm even less
than fiction.

Should I ask one of these guys to go get me a branch
so I can carve a decent child to live in my house?

Should I carve a family from this death and then
bring it to life?

The spirit of this wood is unspeakable.
Pulpsicles

on this day sagging wet as death around us thaws.

Listen to the flesh unbutton a man's name.
Listen to the birds sing over

what he wouldn't take with him to thankful oblivion.

There are thousands of them.
Listen to the rain slap them around. What do they care

now, they are long gone?
All that's left is dead wood for toy makers.

I built a house for them long ago and told them, eat,
and graced them with ending my infinity in death.

They are not like me and for this there is no thanks left,
and if there were, I would want none of it.

I am as sad as Pinocchio's father because I have no child.

Only I am sadder because to bring the wood inside, and
breathe into my work life means that it will happen
again what no one should suffer even once.

Notes

Page 12, "My German 1":
The piano with which I learned to play was a big dark upright named Wilhelm Stein, Berlin. It had been abandoned by the people from whom my parents bought the house. I don't know if it was manufactured in Canada, or brought from Germany by the owners who had migrated to Canada, but I figure it was probably a version of Steinway, which was an American manufacturing company established in the mid-nineteenth century by a German immigrant, Steinweg. Later in the nineteenth-century, Steinweg's sons established a factory in Hamburg. During WW II, the plant in Hamburg was taken over by Nazis for the war effort.

Page 18, "My German 9.2":
The italicized elements in this poem are from Dr. Walter Groß's speech, "National Socialist Racial Policy: A Speech to German Women" delivered at a women's meeting of the National Socialist Party, in October 1934. Notable about this speech is that it never mentions Jews, but establishes the terms that would come to justify the blatant anti-Semitism grounding the Nazi's racial laws. Dr. Groß, "*Nationalsozialistische Rassenpolitik. Eine Rede an die deutschen Frauen* (Dessau, C. Dünnhaupt, 1934). Translated by Randall Bytwerk."

Page 39, "Wall 43":
"*[...] a worldwide war and a war the world will win*" is what Ilich Ramirez Sanchez said about his commitment to the Palestinian cause, at his trial in 1997. Born in Venezuela, Ramirez joined the Palestinian Front for the Liberation of Palestinians (PFLP) after he dropped out of university in

Moscow in 1970. Nicknamed Carlos the Jackal, he terrorized Europe for several decades with assassinations and bombings, until he was caught in 1994 in Sudan by the French police. Convicted for carrying out a triple murder in France in 1975, Carlos received his first life sentence in 1997. In 2011, Carlos received a second life sentence for masterminding four bombings in France in the 1980s.

Page 85, "God's View":
Maruta is the Japanese word for "log"; it was a term used euphemistically by the doctors of the Japanese Imperial Army's Unit 731, to refer to the human test subjects of experimentations.

Acknowledgements

Pieces in this collection previously published include: an earlier version of "Hands 5," under the title, "Al Aqsa Intifada" and "No One," in *Descant: Prisoners* (2010); "Hands 88" under the title, "Violence" in *The Toronto Quarterly, Issue 2* (2009); and a much earlier version of "My German 9.2" under the title, "My German," along with an earlier version of "Frontiers of Construction: Gaza," in *Descant Magazine,* 141 (2008). "Hold" is forthcoming in *The Poet's Quest for God,* anthology edited by Todd Swift, Eyewear Publishing, 2014.

Thanks

This collection has been almost two decades in the making, attesting to its being the product of a labour of love; it also bears the mark of many lovers of poetry who have read and responded to the collection, in part or in whole. Deep and sincere thanks go to all those who have read earlier drafts and incarnations of the poems and the manuscript, over the years. For their feedback and especially their support of my work, I am deeply grateful: Luba Szkambara, Andrea Moodie, Sina Queyras, Martha Hillhouse, Henry Knight, John Oughton, John Donlan, Alana Wilcox, Jay Millar, Noelle Allen and last, but not least, Rob Allen. A special thanks goes to Jason Camlot, the amazing editor of this collection who, not only saw the potential in the ideas I was exploring, but also unknowingly finished a project Rob had started but could not finish before his death, which was to edit this book for publication. Jason's literary sensitivity and his creative responses to my work helped me to discover what I had meant all along, and at critical moments, to point me in the direction of something new. Included in my thanks, as always, are Zaid and Karim, for their patience and love.

Concetta plans to defend her PhD dissertation in the summer of 2013. Her doctoral project in the Humanities Program at York centers on evidence of the trauma of secularism through the iterations of the *objet a* of the messiah and *Muselmann,* in twentieth-century cultural and intellectual works. Her academic work has informed many elements of *walking: Not a Nun's Diary,* as has her work researching, writing and directing for the television documentary series on Biblical archaeology, *The Naked Archaeologist* (2004-7). Her literary publications include a novella, *Stained Glass* (1997) and a collection of prose poems, *Interference* (1999), both with Guernica Editions, as well as publications in Canadian and American literary journals such as *Descant, Exile, Grain, The Malahat Review,* and *Matrix.* She's living in Toronto, doing what she loves.